By the Wreckmaster's Cottage

Paula Rankin

BY THE WRECKMASTER'S COTTAGE

poems

Carnegie-Mellon University Press
Pittsburgh & London 1977

Acknowledgments

Acknowledgment is gratefully made to editors of the following periodicals in which most of these poems first appeared:

Ascent: "Taking Stew to an Old Woman."
Back Door: "Sideshows."
College English: "The Decoy Carver," ©1976 by the National Council of Teachers of English.
Crazy Horse: "Women Partly Explained."
Epos: "On Holding On."
The Lamp in the Spine: "Uncles."
The Nation: "By the Wreckmaster's Cottage at Assateague;" "Furnishing the Past;" "Dunes;" "The Shell-Gatherer;" and "For the Man Who Discovered the New Market Caverns."
North American Review: "Sacrifices."
The Ohio Review: "Family Trees."
Poem: "Riding the Bus;" "Taking All We Can With Us;" "Hazards: Night Driving on Ice;" and "Testing the Ice at Lake Maury."
Poetry Northwest: "Pentecosts;" "In the Ward of Prolonged Care;" "For the Child Last Seen in the Top of Cape Hatteras Lighthouse;" and "To the Ox-Cart Driver."
Prairie Schooner: "To the Boy in the National Geographic Photograph," ©1976 by the University of Nebraska Press.
Shenandoah: "Poem for Actors."
Southern Humanities Review: "Penance."
Southern Poetry Review: "The Catalog People."
Sou'wester: "Notes for the Novel by Everyone;" "To be on a Page Next to Someone You Love;" and "Seven Degrees, at the Beach."
Three Rivers Poetry Journal: "At the Nursing Home;" "On Possibilities;" "Falling in Love for the Nine Millionth Time;" and "The Whittlers."
Westigan Review: "For the Obese;" "Where We Are;" and "Reflections in the Eye Specialist's Waiting Room."

Library of Congress Catalog Card Number: 77-80343
ISBN 0-915604-13-2
Printed and bound in the United States of America
First edition

Contents

IV

I

Poem for Actors

I always wonder what happened
to put them on the far side of the glass,
why they are the channel I watch,
why I am the channel who pays.

I wonder if their mothers rented them
to magazines for models,
if their father knew the president
of something, or if they were simply born
knowing how to walk into a script
and nickname it Life.

I want to know if success
spoiled or redeemed Mary Ann Jones
from life on this side of the screen,
if she still has a nickname she goes by
when using the john like anyone.

I want to plug into their pillows,
to hear what the real dreams say
about rolling so many acts into one,
layers of face we all want to try on
and get paid for, plenty of roles
for an encore, a comeback.

Sideshows

We call them depraved
for what they sell:
Deformity.

We want to say
to the fattest of fat men:
Surely there is something else
you could do
to feed such hunger;
Bearded lady, it would only take a shave.

But then not everyone
can toss fluorescent nipples
and catch them easily as coins
or display the ambiguities of his sex
unabashed. Perhaps these too are callings?

If you have enough quarters,
they will show you everything
you'd only guessed at
from Hermaphrodite's shadow
on the side of the tent
to the glassed-in fetus
of a beast child who,
if he never sees his cut
of suckers' money,
will live as long as a memory
when the canvas drops
and its tenants slip into trucks
leaving the fields full of squashed cups
but no trail

though we go back for days
with more quarters.

Pentecosts

We're told the Apostles
on that day
bloomed swirls of fire
like lit junipers
right out of their brains.
Because we cannot imagine a man,
much less twelve, on fire
and happy about it,
we take this story with a grain of salt
which under microscope would show up
as many grains of envy.

Under microscope envy would be
broken down into tiny mirrors
that reflect us, rubbing sticks
to spark any number of flames,
using our heads like match-ends
to strike dialogues between ourselves
and all we cannot reach by word of mouth—
the dog warming his bones in the sun,
the cricket with so much to say
and no one to translate,
the sounds of trees growing at night,
and each other: the unspoken under microscope
looping the body's limbs to the brain,
a constant simmering brushfire
that keeps us going
as long as there's something to burn.

Under microscope
all the cells want in.
They all want to burn
and be happy about it.

To the Boy in the National Geographic Photograph

By now you have pedaled out of the picture
which, for you, has no edges,
only cobblestones linking real lives,
real respiratory systems churning
their share of thatched air.

Yet you stare at me
as if this picture meant more
than a photographer's promise of coins
for holding still, for wiring your eyes
through Kodachrome to the unfilmed nights
in which we really live.

Between us, oceans crash and withdraw,
leaving shells whose tenants
are always vanishing. It is from inside
a shell that I write you this poem,
praising our stares through windows,
mirrors, a camera's lens, any aim
toward each other's eyes.

Women Partly Explained

Wind waits for stillness,
a settling down of things.
There is this air that nests
in tree   houses   faces of women
numb with inhaling the unchanging rooms
of their lives. It has something to do
with prime cuts of meat,
with the teeth of husbands and children,
with
     Indians
          tracking
who do not imagine
wood broken down into tables and chairs
who slit open our sleep
like an animal's skin,
their eyes glazed with soft smoke from piñon
where it breaks into prayers for the gods
who mate in the core of the sun,

our dreams the only shelter they have found.

For the Obese

We are always saying,
with will power,
their buttons would slip into holes
over their bellies, their zippers
would close like a mouth
which gets the last word
in the old argument
of why some eat to stay alive
while some eat to summon impossible lovers
who fill every inch of the body.

Then we say it's hard to find their eyes
or the stand their bones take
so far underground.
We lock them into their bodies,
slipping the key into our pocket,
fingering it from time to time
as reminder of those few wars
we aren't a part of.

Uncles

They say it's usually someone
you'd least suspect

Someone who knows all the names
of your children
and where each soft spot
dips into each delicate head

Listen to the glove rummage
inside the toy chest

Someone is knocking
Someone is always knocking
That sweet face
stuffed in his pocket like candy

Riding the Bus

We climb on, dropping tokens,
pieces of our lives
where they glint in the meter
like fillings from teeth,
repaired pavements for meals
of guilt or good intentions.

The advertisements arch into themselves
as if some great truth
were leaning against them,
forcing them to feed forever
on their own lies.

Our pooled breathing is unintelligible.
We could be moving through water
like the newly drowned,
floating up to the place
of new beginnings, the movie
that starts when we get there.
We save our voices for this.

Streets climb up to the windows
then fall off, like half-hearted attempts
of a burglar not sure
he needs to include us.
We settle into the fog of ourselves
while a great motor pushes
the bothersome details out the exhausts,
leaving landscapes as smeared as our pasts.

The Catalog People

Their eyes stay pinned
to something off the page,
as if trying to track their own flesh
drained from sweaters and pants.
A girl in tricot pretends lust
while brassieres deflate
like unfilled orders. The shoes dream
of tracking us into our lives;
furs hoard what little they remember
of beasthood and human blood.

When we slap down their sky
locking them into their sizes
we refuse to imagine their moving
through pages like rooms
swapping tales of our lives.

Taking All We Can With Us

It's always something overlooked,
the monogrammed stick-pin left
on the ledge, the footprint in wet
cement beyond the door where someone
ran screaming, Thief!

Of course we are no more thieves
than anyone who steals
from each unguarded entry
that keeps trying to break into print
as Chapter I of novels we lug through our heads.

Even dust tells a story: it has only two
lives, swirling and landing,
and it lands only on the left-too-long,
the plate never thrown, the chair
never sat in, the face
never twisted in anguish or love.

Moving is our way of confusing the dust,
of convincing ourselves that much
is still unsettled, that we still
have some say in our endings. Sometimes
we even dream there is nothing
we cannot take with us, that we will be first
to perform the real vanishing act.
Even signatures on checks will dissolve
and fly with us for identity.
We will know
and be known
by all we can carry.

There will be nothing to auction or bequest.

II

Sacrifices

Staring into the mammoth's fossilized jaw,
I think of all the holes
where we never touch bottom,
cannonballs through civil war soldiers,
gaps left by abominable snowmen
crossing over.

When I touch the spearhead lodged
in his backbone, I remember Indians
gored through their pectoral muscles
with the same weapon, sacrificed to all the gods
who counted: sun, wind, river, rain.
Now here we all come as tourists, pretending
to watch from such distance, planting ourselves
like crops that need no intervention.

Last night I watched a dog
bleed for hours after death,
the god of ignitions satisfied, spinning rubber
towards other intersections

and I found myself asking
whether willingness counts, if the cells
must announce their intention
before they meet tire, razor, bullet,
or a bridge's cement pilings,
if the body must make its leap
with all the pores open

or if getting pushed counts
or even being nudged, lash-blink
by lash-blink, towards the edge
something's always slipping off of.

By the Wreckmaster's Cottage at Assateague

The dunes loosen like winding sheets
and with them all hope
of keeping things covered:
grains at the time, they ride the bay wind
and start over wherever they land.

Slowly the sand releases the boats
to new owners: keel, spar, masthead
jabbed towards sky like the finger of blame.
I run my hand over ribs picked clean
by men who are always arriving first
at scenes of disaster, sifting through bones
for lockets, daguerreotype grins, strands
of hair stripped white by drinking
last thoughts from drowned brains.

I think of passengers huddled in holds
dreaming of impenetrable cypress
like an ark nothing chews through,
of what it must be to go down
in full view of the light
on Assateague Island

like any landlubber,
like those of us who keep falling
through hyphenated light
until sand weaves the coat
that will fit us.

At the Nursing Home

I always find him riding their leatherette
sofa through the lobby
into his book's landscape.

The window faces those who use their legs
to push a clutch or gas or brakes.
I have never caught him

moving through that window
in a daydream
where roads snail our past

into our future, and the present
lives only as long as it takes
for a light to turn green.

The puzzle I've never seen him work
lies half-finished on a card table,
its sky interlocking with river

and pieces of trees.
Our visits are timed
by the scissors of a clock's face

wedging his days into naps,
meals, contacts with the world I bring
merely by walking
and talking to pictures of me
on his glasses.

Furnishing the Past

The problem is what to do with so much space
where no one we know has ever been.
All we have to go on are old tables
and chairs, sidewalks that jump
the curled yellow border
clamped on lives
by the camera's click.

Because we cannot,
we want to enter their bodies
taking part in whatever moves them
to windows and doors and each other
while an 1890 maple rakes air
into the twentieth century
and a deeper kind of shadow prints
bushes, bricks, the space
where our faces begin.

The Riders

"They are paid more for the roller coaster ride, as wages are
related to risk"—excerpt from blurb on the movie **Roller Coaster**

When the switch is flicked on,
we begin screaming

for the hell of it, making up
for dummies they've packed

into other seats, their rubber mouths
molded into shapes movie-goers

will pay to claim as their own. At least
when you get paid, you know

what disaster awaits you, though
the worth of this knowledge

is debatable. From the top
to the bottom of steel that only seems

to bend predictably, we ride
for everyone whose heart arrests

when the octopus whirls its fifty
arms, each stuffed with lovers, children,

or those who simply break stride
and toss their lives at the mercy

of giant motors. Three minutes
and we're due to crash

through the fake balsa-wood front
of the House of Mirrors

where sheets of wavy glass
wait for arms, legs, faces to fall

into all the shapes that swell inside us
when we try to enter someone else.

But now the mirrors only lean
like old people in nursing homes,

full of stories they don't know
how to pass on to each other,

strange eyes that balloon
as we come into focus.

In the Ward of Prolonged Care

Beyond these windows men are dying fast,
while here tubes plug men into the system
of pulse and spare time mapped between
each stroke and false alarm. Each man
has had enough time to have turned Buddhist,
guru, Adam, or Moses checking slabs
for comma splices.

I too am plugged into a system
which pulses me to be prepared,
and I will be, if spared these months
of second-guessing, with my head wired
to outstare a ceiling, while blood strings
someone else's veins and mine throb
in full recognition of the loan.

On Possibilities

The idea of having lived before:
fresh tracks in my mind's jungle
where ape still calls to ape

and the subconscious' vines
feed on anything—
if truth lies there

it is a myna bird
with too many voices
or ptarmigan dying

of its own camouflaged color.
When I think of what we cannot know
except by going there

that birds are everywhere—
we pick one's plumage
for our own

and dedicate the wings we never had
to winds that strip our skins
even as we pray.

Taking Stew to an Old Woman

She lets me in and I offer the leavings
of yesterday's stew, disguised
in a bright yellow bowl.
I do not know her, know only facts
eyes and ears sponge from a distance:
she is old, alone, and nights her porch light
flushes the dark from my bedroom.
I do not tell her of times I have stared
at her half-open slats for eyes
that must, by now, have trained themselves
to ride venetian blinds like a bumpless road
where each traveler lands safely home.

She sets the bowl on a table, explaining
how this room once was the parlor,
how her bed is in the dining room,
how her cupboard creaks less now that she cooks
in the bedroom. Is this what it comes to,
I think, a reconstruction of rooms,
a scrambling of knobs, plates, photographs,
as if the eye might be fooled,
the walls tricked into utter confusion?

Yet nothing seems moved: someone has sprayed
an aerosol can of fine dust. I sit
because she asks me to, because I sense need
like a bottle I found once in the ocean:
the note must have floated for years,
its owner needing me way before then.
I listen to tales of husband and sons
strung out like wash on a clothesline,
limp sleeves almost filling with air.
All the while I am facing her bed,
open as a boat under ceiling.

It has been handed down
through the family, she says

none of whom is present
when an 86-year-old woman
takes out her teeth,
tries hard for her bones
to make some impression
as she slips between sheets
and prays for the dead.

I wonder if I stayed long enough
could I ask my real questions:
how far from me to you?
How to turn loss
into small acts of levitation,
short floats between mattress and ceiling?

I go through the motions of leaving,
my best act, knowing I walk behind her
as I go down the steps. She flicks on
her porch light again

where each night the moths singe their wings
while she rearranges the smallest of rooms,
rescattering the objects of attention
like the rest of us who pray
for the dead and the living.

III

Hazards: Night Driving on Ice

That night even the ocean stopped
keeping time by tides and froze its collection
of beer cans, shells, bottles stuffed
too late with calls for help.

Then I did not think to ask
whether everyone deludes himself
that he has left in the nick of time?
Perhaps there were others
similarly caught that night
without warning, leaping from barstools,
sofas, beds, into coats, cars, praying
road crews had salted their particular
treads through ice—

but to us they were only
a Buick flipped on its side
a station wagon crunched on a guard rail
lanes packed with the world's worst
skaters, drivers who had no training in skids;

to us they were only wrecks
forecasting shapes we must choose from.
That night the Exxon station
locked its pumps, unplugged its neon flash
like a yanked promise, and we had to ignite
a tank of almost nothing, slide out
on treadless tires
and the blizzard blew into my head,
each microscopic crystal dissolving its
whisper: Now you will learn to be good.

You turned on the radio
and it was snowing there too
all over the songs of true, false,
open, secret, calm, frantic, platonic,
incestuous, right and wrong

Loves, all over each larynx, diaphragm,
nasal twang that swore fidelity
inside the grooves of scratched records.

You thought I was eating my hand.
I was praying
as only the guilt-ridden can
that we were some halfway-fallen angel's
special assignment, that your hands
on the steering wheel, tires spinning
towards home were last chances
for earning wings back.

Long since home,
safely unpacked with one of the stories
of minor disaster that keeps our lives
salvageable, only now do I dare
to look back
for your face
behind the windshield wipers,
your eyes filling/emptying
with blizzard/love

only now do I think to ask
if everyone brings with himself to a window
steamed vision, an inability to wipe stares
clean when aiming them backwards,
salt drifting like snow through the bloodstream,

Lot's wife alive
though hardly well,
hardly breathing.

Penance

Hating what I have become,
I leave the house
as if walking out of my body,
in search of other shells
whose tenants have vanished.

A cat tears trout from yesterday's garbage,
leaving a week's waste spread all over
the yard. I hiss with the guilt
I want him to feel, the leap
that would leave his fur
free for the taking.

I watch a caterpillar chewing his way
through my leaves, a tube of sun
and chlorophyll, all of his legs tracking
the veins where wings grow.
When I try to blow judgment like hurricane
through his pores, the space
where my shoulder blades used to be throbs.

All day I track ants, starlings, squirrels,
a dog warming his bones in the sun,
neighbors' sleeves that flap
whatever wind tells them, finding nothing
ready to trade its vascular system for mine
and I know I will have to climb
back into my body, hoping new orders
will come down from wind to my bones,
hoping the body can be blown into other stances
besides the one it keeps now behind the window,
balancing a face
that has not let me out of its sight.

Notes for the Novel by Everyone

Tonight wind breaks like ocean
through trees, limbs crack, adding
dead wood to the house's pile of brick.
All holes in the house are found out:
flue in the chimney, fan for sucking odors,
cracked pane in the attic, sliver of night
at the base of the door,
tempering movements under wattage.

Perfect for the Gothic novel
we've constructed for our lives,
the starring role we play in all our stories.

The wind comes a long way to find us.
Like torn branches, we wait, the sap
still coursing our veins, a few shoots
still inexplicably green.

Dunes

It is always their season
for change, open as they are
to wind from any direction.
Climbing them, we sense how few
shaping breaths have shaped us,
having battened down our lives
for hurricane, ignoring all minor winds
beyond which our real living stands,
sculpted, as if out of stone.

Only the dune remains open.
Our feet sink their trails in its sand.

On Holding On

All the proof we need,
waiting in our book of picture squares.
Children that were you and I
squared off with popsicles dripping,
baseballs gloved,
skirts hanging, pants bagging,
flipping pages,
holding on—

Pants and skirts stop their sagging
Taking shape on bodies taking
shape
Swells, bulges, spreads
locked up in flatness
as we in our bursting bodies
were flatly guessing about
how to enter our lives:
smiles of secret knowledge
from passed around books
and wet pants.

Turning slowly now,
We know these faces better;
we search the eyes instead.
Friends, glass-eyed, grinning,
glasses held in toasts,
picnic tables, Christmas trees,
the burlesque of it all
is making us smile,
so that later,
eyes will not matter;

We can say, Here it is!
Look! We were laughing

Now we train the children
that are ours
Look at the man now
Smile at his hand
One   two   three
Here it is!
Look!
You are smiling
You are happy here with us
Come into the picture book

Falling in Love for the Nine Millionth Time

for Scott

Wind always wants us somewhere else:
but once in a while
we stand firm, becoming leaves
that fall through the loosening air
behind eyes.

Soon enough, snow
and always the wind.
Soon enough we go
where wind wants us to go.

To be on a Page Next to Someone You Love

To be on a page next to someone you love
is at least something. What fraction
of tree are two pages, what fraction
of all combinations of type?
Page, you are my hand inside the closed book,
scaling his print as if it were beard.
You are my face pressed against stained glass.

Inside the slammed sky of books,
our words pull up easier chairs
than those our bodies sat in.
Now there is not even skin between us.

Seven Degrees, at the Beach

The ocean has more chances.
What do we expect, coming back?
To come upon those summer bodies
still wielding the homemade geiger counter
over the sand, eyes on the soaring meter?
Don't you remember, all we dug up
were bottle caps or empty cans,
rarely small change. All day
for a nickel. I knew then
we'd never be rich.

Now whatever the ocean has to say
has only to wait on another weather.
As I watch you wait for me
the closest I can come
is up to this roof of me,
this underside of ice: memory.
Oh I remember the pounding
of this ocean, the promise
of buried treasure at our feet;
I hoard these down here,
where I live.

But what good new weather?
I am no kinsman of water.

Testing the Ice at Lake Maury

Beyond skeletal trees the live oak
flushes space with leaves green
as what I remember of baseball caps
bobbing on heads here last summer.
Tonight the only game is with nets,
with guessing how deep the ice goes
in Virginia, where salt is always at work
inside water, thawing each unguaranteeable footing
in less time than it takes
for a man to put on his skates
and go down

as if searching games called off
by summer rain, sure wins
denied us by weather.

Always I am the one without skates
who steps out as if shoes
buckled a sure-footed faith
in planked water,
though when I look back
there is only a stone lion
keeping watch the way the sculpted
or dead do
and I know again
the dread of depending
on my own myopic vision,
the squint I must master
to measure the thickness between feet
and fish holding so still at the bottom
even they do not dream they are saved.

I throw a fistful of rocks
and walk towards scars, wondering at branches

sealed beneath the ice, if they were planted
for the drowned to climb in
and stare back at suckers
like me. I admit it, I am one,

but God, how I keep coming back,
retracing whatever zero can freeze
of the blood, swearing it was here
I tossed the path to wisdom

with a sinker on it,
wondering what makes me think I can find it
again, its spine still intact, if only
I am granted enough time
on the top side of ice.

Where We Are

I think it's the way
you moved through your life:
as if you were no one at all.

I never saw gray become anyone;
on you it was a silver shirt
I watched moving in and out
of the classroom, into your car,
down the right hand side of the road,
straight. Home free by 10:15.

Oh, I am no one too,
but that's another address.
It will still be me calling your name
from the top of the roller coaster,
waiting for the conductor to show up
to ask for my ticket
to throw me off when he discovers
I never bought one.

We come together in the middle of a forest,
not convincing each other
that either method of travel is best;
certain only that we move,
that we meet,
warm hands before a fire,
set out again to clear our small paths
like no one, no one at all.

Reflections in the Eye Specialist's Waiting Room

Here we are,
the people who do not see well.
There is no talk;
I pass the time blurring people's faces.
They are mostly old men.
I am called next;
I have drops put in my eyes.
I ask, will it stop burning?
I am given a tissue,
told to go back and wait.
I think, now would be such a safe
time to cry—
I will bite myself when no one is looking.
Instead, wishing I had worn a calf-length skirt
all the way down the hall where
old men are watching me come back,
I return, sit in a different chair.
I get out a cigarette and a book of matches.
I strike.
It is not until I try to make contact
between the two
that I am afraid:
my eyes cannot find the lighting point.
Between it and the flame is the
Old Woman,
the one I have seen in mirrors,
looking down the road of my face.

I slam my eyes and burn her.

I inhale.

IV

The Shell-Gatherer

At Ocracoke, I met a woman
who stayed on long after others
had ferried to mainland winters,
leaving boats and shops slammed
against tourists
and the hungry wind.

She stayed to ferret low tides alone,
when the ocean, cleaning house,
dumps its dustpan of expendables:
dwellings whose tenants have drowned
into new lives as shark cells,
fish eyes, gull feathers.

We combed seaweed,
wondering at the nutritional value of snarls
tossed at our feet by hurricane
and tidal wave. She chose only whole shells,
cupping oceans to her ear
like Anglo-Saxon riddles,
nicknaming each conch and Scotch-bonnet,
explaining drained lives,
how the animals buffed their walls
with their bodies to get that shine.

Most were chewed by wind
and salt water, but some held like whorled opals,
as if there are skins no element can scour.
Deep in mainland freezings, I still see
the old woman, barnacled to tides and silt,
shelling a dream for the rest of us
of flesh beneath pores, of polishing
our lives from inside out
as if no elements conspired
to shake themselves clean of us.

For the Child Last Seen in the Top of Cape Hatteras Lighthouse

Child, I have come from the dunes
where all day I practiced the scaling
of sand, that unpracticeable trick
of leaning the body against grains
that shift with each shape of wind.

I have come, tracking the small, salted
wind of your breath like a rumor
beneath which wives of fisherman toss
their dry lives, a rumor only fins survive
and crustaceans repeat to themselves

as they molt under rocks, between shells.
Child, I am inside that tower's one
circular wall, my hand on corrosion for balance,
on illegible letters chalked by those
who climbed this coiled stairwell

when a light throbbed back at the moon,
pulling men home against waves. It is
from inside that light that I call you,
impossibly persuading you down from your dream
of becoming an angel, back into the air

of those left among us still sane,
those who mix breaths only with wings
a wind beats through the lungs,
under the armpits, over feet
planted firmly in sand.

To the Ox-Cart Driver

Stropping oxen, you nudge through town
with bedsprings, bottles, chimney bricks,
riding the rumor that there are always men
who'll try anything on.

I stare into ox eyes
that scald me with their dumbness,
their blank recognition of road
and burden, their disregard
for the changing directions of wind.

You hold up your collections
of drained sleeves, pants, shoes,
telling me how washing will shrink
them to fit. I do not say

how it is ox I want to barter for,
how I need to try on hide blunt-nosing its way
through the dark without questioning,
until yokes press as lightly on skin
as a shirt passed down
from hand to hand to hand.

The Decoy Carver

Once I was the best
at hearing the pulse inside logs,
at timing my scalpel to uncover wings,
feathers, eyes that go on staring.
Now cataracts cloud the passage of light,
forcing me to look where lash-blinks
provide no intermission. God knows

where they came from, those men
with new orders each season
for dead-ringers, for shapes I guaranteed
would lure the ones with breath
into range, a money-back-if-not-satisfied
month of bagging. Then there were others
who pleaded orders I could not fill:
human faces pricked down to last details
of pore. I pretended not to hear their wish
to be shown my private collection, grain
even I could not tell from real men and women,
the warp I could not pound from pine.

How many nights I have lain here
and dreamed my intended vocation: an itinerant fakir
recarving only new shapes for his body,
a worker of wonders in skin,
deceptions so sleek you'd never guess
how long I've honed and waited for real wings
to notice me, how often
I've tried to lure you here
with nothing but the brain's bag
of pitiable tricks, dull knives

guessing at measurements, at final proportions.

The Whittlers

No decoy-carvers, these. Here it is enough
that a man saves his knife for the plainest
of sticks, not seeking the cumbersome shapes
that clog pine. Besides, their business
has more to do with shavings
than with mythical points at which wood
becomes something other: these are the experts
on how to make nothing

but stories, each chip a distortion
of shapes seen through fog.
Hindsight is everything to them.
One, thumbless, tells again
of missing the blind spot between a crab's
stalked eyes, of learning too late
the mosaics crabs make
out of anyone's bare hand.

The others nod, take turns cursing
the mystery of catches, swear nothing would make them
go back. They are all liars. But they know it
in ways we do not,

we who give them a bench
in the center of town, hewing our own breaths
from fog, bent on the making of shapes
that will show we have been here.
They do not know how we watch them
shaving sticks.

For the Man Who Discovered the New Market Caverns

Now the caverns are wired
so the guide can flick on sections of wall
still damp from wearing centuries of river
like a skin. I half listen as he points
to stone organs, bridal chambers,
keeping my inner ear pressed
to the work of the water,
its patient unwinding through stone.

Going down, I try not to think
of the way you descended, your body's ride
through darkest lovers' tunnels.
Finally I kneel and stare down a hole
with no bottom, with not even a flashlight
to pick up the pulse of black water
on its slash downward, the gills
of blind fish bloated with eggs.
I press my ear to that current, listening
for a new way of breathing
you may have picked up by drowning,

something I can carry back
besides these chunks of stalactite
that take more than our lives
dripping into columns.
Even now I dream your mastering strokes
for all of us who walk out onto floors
we always assume will be there,
our waterlogged cells bucking the odds
at the bottom, taking in river,
gargling back bubbles of air.

For the Ferryman in the Chesapeake Tunnel

You must be eighty. When I was a child
you were old enough to appear as ogre
in stories we made up waiting for the ferry
to bear us to Gloucester. You'd pick us
from the rails, make us stand
behind chains, warning how the bay
only pretended withholding,
how water always had its way.

Now you lean in a booth
and stare out as if stunned
by the dryness of exhausts, carbon, skin,
by our means of moving through water.

Keep Up Speed, the signs say,
and we do, engines churning us
towards blinding slots of light
with only you to stop us.
Here, while ocean goes about its business
of wearing down hulls, sailors, tunnel wall,
no one snores, shuffles a deck,
barters with vendors for fish.

Yet behind my windshield I am still riding
the ferry, old prophet, half expecting
you to step from your booth
and flag us down, stating wind's
velocity, the pull of undertow.
Is there nothing of which you can warn us,
some skiff gone down, a body washing up
at Hatteras, sunbathers gathering
to identify the drowned?
Speak now, while we can turn around
and go back where we came from,
more than willing to learn second-hand
fees charged at the end of the tunnel.

55

Family Trees

For each one trunked to presidents
or Oscar-winners, there's another
twigged to uncles who could whistle,
cousins thin as leaf-veins,
where closet skeletons farm feudal plots
through the darkest of ages.
Once dead, each lives again
through telltale warts or high blood
pressure, pounding against
the second death of history.

From one of them an acorn drops
from which will rise a Southern Baptist
Pope, some unforgettable first
of its line, while the rest coagulate
on branches, scratching epitaphs
on the loosely packed air.

Lighthouses: Odds Concerning Rescue

To really know them, you'd have to row
from island to island: Bloodworth, Barren,
Tangier, Assateague. It would be best
if you'd sprung a leak
but did not know it,
if your sense of direction aimed you
through clouds laid on water, fog rowing
as close as one can to real shipwreck.

Only by seeing them poke at odd-angles
from moss-covered stones, jagged scraps
of oyster shells, their pilings corkscrewed
into the muck of shoal water,
could you begin to suspect
how much they are a matter of trust
betrayed: smashed windows, rusted-out ladders
to cages of light, holes where wedges of stone

once wound from ashes of Indians' graves
to lanterns of flame, as if reversing
what they could of a process. Yet they lean
as if still keeping watch
for one going down in a bugeye, trawler, scow,
maybe you in the flimsiest of rowboats,
where you could have sworn
unautomated flash just glanced your forearm,
picking up the heart's thumps for help.

Farther inland, on the main street
of Chincoteague, there is a mission
where drunks go
for salvation, coffee, the soup of the day

which is the same every day
except for the addition of water,
a gradual, relentless thinning down
of nutriments slurped into bodies.

Here, after repentance, they wait
for the hurricane power rumored to swell
in second winds. To blur the waiting,
they swap amnesias, distortions
of former repairs, how it felt
to go down
and come up
nailing legs on discarded tables, knobs

on stuck drawers, rebuilding failed
Bendix motors, in a room where all junk
is dreamed salvageable.
With heads full of hammers, paint scrapers,
nails, no one recalls how many times
he's been saved, what bar's on-off neon flash
did not give up
until it found him.
It is from here that the wind
begins its collection of rumors,
then shifts toward ocean, spends its life
feeling for a place to lie down in,

that stretch of untended shoreline
dividing the hopeful
from the hopeless,
that hole into which all ropes are tossed
from structures that lean, crumble, keep watch

through slits mortar abandoned
when stairwells funneled light
with human keepers,

cones of kerosene
going down
coming up in the oddest places
eyes   ribcages   windows
by which women sit
long after dark,
refusing the grim statistics,
waiting for someone like you.

Carnegie-Mellon Poetry

The Living and the Dead, Ann Hayes (1975)
In the Face of Descent, T. Alan Broughton (1975)
The Week the Dirigible Came, Jay Meek (1976)
Full of Lust and Good Usage, Stephen Dunn (1976)
How I Escaped from the Labyrinth
  and Other Poems, Philip Dacey (1977)
The Lady from the Dark Green Hills, Jim Hall (1977)
For Luck: Poems 1962-1977, H. L. Van Brunt (1977)
By the Wreckmaster's Cottage, Paula Rankin (1977)

Books in the Carnegie-Mellon University Press Poetry Series
are distributed by the University of Pittsburgh Press,
127 N. Bellefield Avenue, Pittsburgh Pennsylvania 15260.